MASTI
THE KOREAN
ALPHABET

MW00889616

A Handwriting Practice Workbook

Perfect your calligraphy skills and
dominate the Hangul script

by Lang Workbooks

Important Legal Information:

ISBN: 9781650817460

ㅈ

지읒
JIEUT

ﾉ

Stroke Order

1
2
3

Example Syllables

잠 좐 재
쟌 접 좨

Clear large letters make it easy to recognize even the most detailed characters.

Approximate Pronunciation

- **INITIAL:** SIMILAR TO THE "CH" IN "**CHAIR**"
- **FINAL:** "T" AS IN "OU**T**"

- IPA: /tɕ/
- IPA: /t̚/

Detailed instructions provide you with a strong foundation to build up your handwriting and pronunciation skills.

Trace and Learn

ㅈ ㅈ ㅈ ㅈ ㅈ ㅈ ㅈ ㅈ

mple Font riations

Dedicated sections are designed to imprint proper stroke technique unto your muscle memory.

Pro tip: Go through the first row of each letter and familiarize yourself with the stroke order of each basic shape before tackling the more challenging syllables, composed of various shapes, on the following rows.

Font variations train your brain to recognize alternative character styles.

As a bonus, at the end of this workbook you'll find training pages for the high-frequency syllables. Feel free to photocopy these pages as needed to extend the lifetime value of your workbook.

Workbook Index

ㄱ

기역

GIYEOK

G

감 관 개

삭 긱 괘

Approximate Pronunciation

- **INITIAL:** "G" AS IN "GO"
- **FINAL:** "C" AS IN "DOCTOR"

- IPA: /g/
- IPA: /k̚/

Trace and Learn

ㄱ ㄱ ㄱ ㄱ ㄱ ㄱ ㄱ ㄱ ㄱ ㄱ

ㄱ ㄱ ㄱ ㄱ ㄱ ㄱ ㄱ ㄱ ㄱ

가 가 가 가 가 가 가 가 가

공 공 공 공 공 공 공 공

경 경 경 경 경 경 경 경 경 경

Example Font Variations

ㄱ
ㄱ
ㄱ
ㄱ

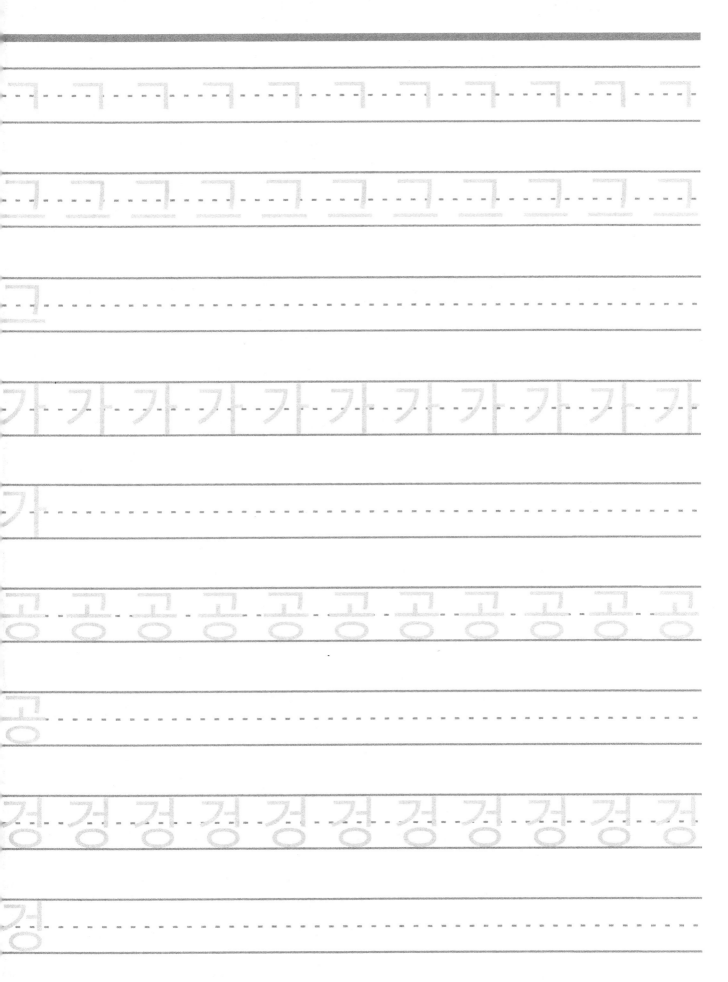

ㄲ

쌍기역
Ssanggieok

Kk

깜 꽌 깨
깐 꼅 꽤

- **INITIAL:** SIMILAR TO THE "C" IN "CAT" BUT WITH A TENSER THROAT.
- **FINAL:** "C" AS IN "DOCTOR"

- IPA: /k̚/
- IPA: /k͈/

ㄲ — ㄲ — ㄲ — ㄲ — ㄲ — ㄲ — ㄲ — ㄲ — ㄲ — ㄲ — ㄲ

ㄲ — ㄲ — ㄲ — ㄲ — ㄲ — ㄲ — ㄲ — ㄲ — ㄲ — ㄲ — ㄲ

ㄲ --

까 — 까 — 까 — 까 — 까 — 까 — 까 — 까 — 까 — 까 — 까

까 --

꼬 꼬 꼬 꼬 꼬 꼬 꼬 꼬 꼬 꼬 꼬
ㅇ ㅇ ㅇ ㅇ ㅇ ㅇ ㅇ ㅇ ㅇ ㅇ ㅇ

꼬 --
ㅇ

껑 껑 껑 껑 껑 껑 껑 껑 껑 껑 껑
ㅇ ㅇ ㅇ ㅇ ㅇ ㅇ ㅇ ㅇ ㅇ ㅇ ㅇ

껑 --
ㅇ

ㄴ

니은
SSANGGIEOK

N

남 놘 내
놘 녑 놰

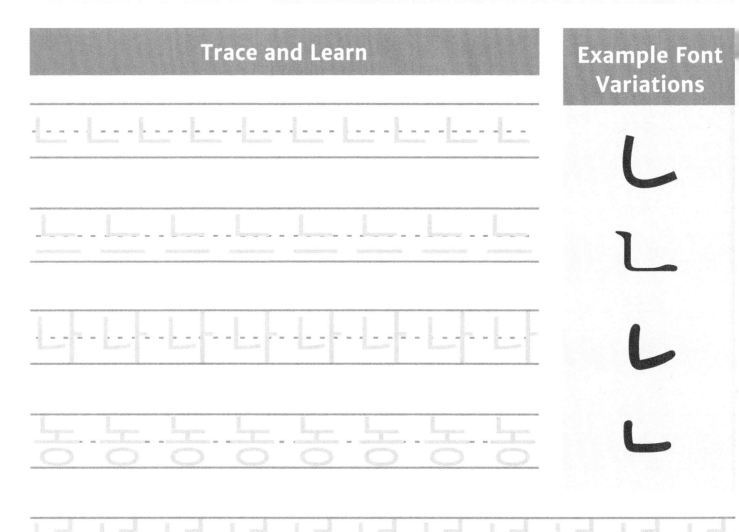

Approximate Pronunciation

- **INITIAL:** "N" AS IN "**N**OW"
- **FINAL:** "N" AS IN "**N**OW"

- IPA: /n/
- IPA: /n/

Trace and Learn

Example Font Variations

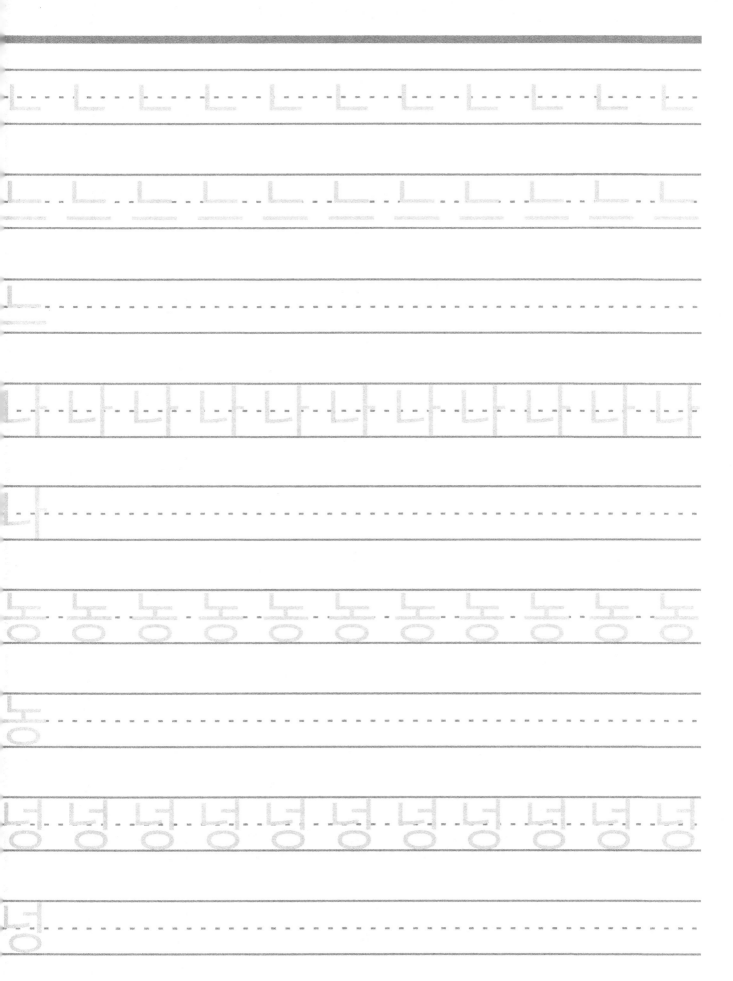

ㄷ

디귿
DIKEUT

D

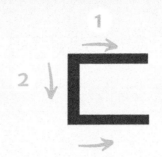

담 돤 대
단 뎝 돼

Approximate Pronunciation

- **INITIAL:** "T" AS IN "**T**IME"
- **FINAL:** "T" AS IN "OU**T**"

- IPA: / t /
- IPA: / t̚ /

Trace and Learn

Example Font Variations

ㄷ
ㄷ
ㄷ
ㄷ

ㄷ ㄷ ㄷ ㄷ ㄷ ㄷ ㄷ ㄷ ㄷ ㄷ ㄷ ㄷ

ㄷ ㄷ ㄷ ㄷ ㄷ ㄷ ㄷ ㄷ ㄷ ㄷ ㄷ

ㄷ

다 다 다 다 다 다 다 다 다 다 다 다

다

도 도 도 도 도 도 도 도 도 도
ㅇ ㅇ ㅇ ㅇ ㅇ ㅇ ㅇ ㅇ ㅇ ㅇ

ㅇ

도 도 도 도 도 도 도 도 도 도
ㅇ ㅇ ㅇ ㅇ ㅇ ㅇ ㅇ ㅇ ㅇ ㅇ

동

ㄸ

쌍디귿
SSANGDIKEUT

Tt

1 3
2 4

땀 똔 때
딴 떱 뙈

Approximate Pronunciation

- **INITIAL:** SIMILAR TO THE "T" IN "TIME" BUT WITH A TENSER THROAT.
- **FINAL:** -

- IPA: / t̤ /
- IPA: / - /

Trace and Learn

ㄸ ㄸ ㄸ ㄸ ㄸ ㄸ ㄸ ㄸ ㄸ ㄸ

ㄸ ㄸ ㄸ ㄸ ㄸ ㄸ ㄸ ㄸ

따 따 따 따 따 따 따 따

또 또 또 또 또 또 또 또

떠 떠 떠 떠 떠 떠 떠 떠 떠

Example Font Variations

ㄸ
ㄸ
ㄸ
ㄸ

ㄹ

리을
RIEUL

R, L

람 롼 래
럴 렵 뢔

Approximate Pronunciation

- **INITIAL:** "Tt" as in "Better"
- **FINAL:** "L" as in "Love"

- IPA: / ɾ /
- IPA: / l /

Trace and Learn

Example Font Variations

ㄹ
ㄹ
ㄹ
ㄹ

ㄹ ㄹ ㄹ ㄹ ㄹ ㄹ ㄹ ㄹ ㄹ ㄹ ㄹ ㄹ

ㄹ ㄹ ㄹ ㄹ ㄹ ㄹ ㄹ ㄹ ㄹ ㄹ ㄹ ㄹ

료

라 라 라 라 라 라 라 라 라 라 라 라

라

로 로 로 로 로 로 로 로 로 로
ㅇ ㅇ ㅇ ㅇ ㅇ ㅇ ㅇ ㅇ ㅇ ㅇ

를
애

려 려 려 려 려 려 려 려 려 려 려
ㅇ ㅇ ㅇ ㅇ ㅇ ㅇ ㅇ ㅇ ㅇ ㅇ

려
ㅇ

미음
MIEUM

M

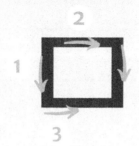

맘 먠 매
먄 몁 뫠

Approximate Pronunciation

- **INITIAL:** "M" AS IN "MORE"
- **FINAL:** "M" AS IN "MORE"

- IPA: /m/
- IPA: /m/

Trace and Learn

Example Font Variations

16

ㅂ

비읍
BIEUP

B

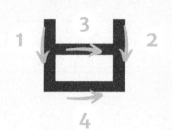

1
3
2
4

Example Syllables

밤 봔 배
반 볍 봬

Approximate Pronunciation

- **INITIAL:** "B" AS IN "BE"
- **FINAL:** "P" AS IN "PUT"

- IPA: /b/
- IPA: /p/

Trace and Learn

Example Font Variations

ㅂ
ㅂ
ㅂ
ㅂ

ᄈ

쌍비읍

SSANGBIEUP

Pp

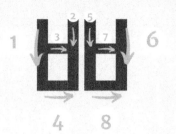

밤 빤 빼
빤 뱁 빼

- **INITIAL:** SIMILAR TO THE "P" IN "PUT" BUT WITH A TENSER THROAT.
- **FINAL:** -

- IPA: /p͈/
- IPA: / - /

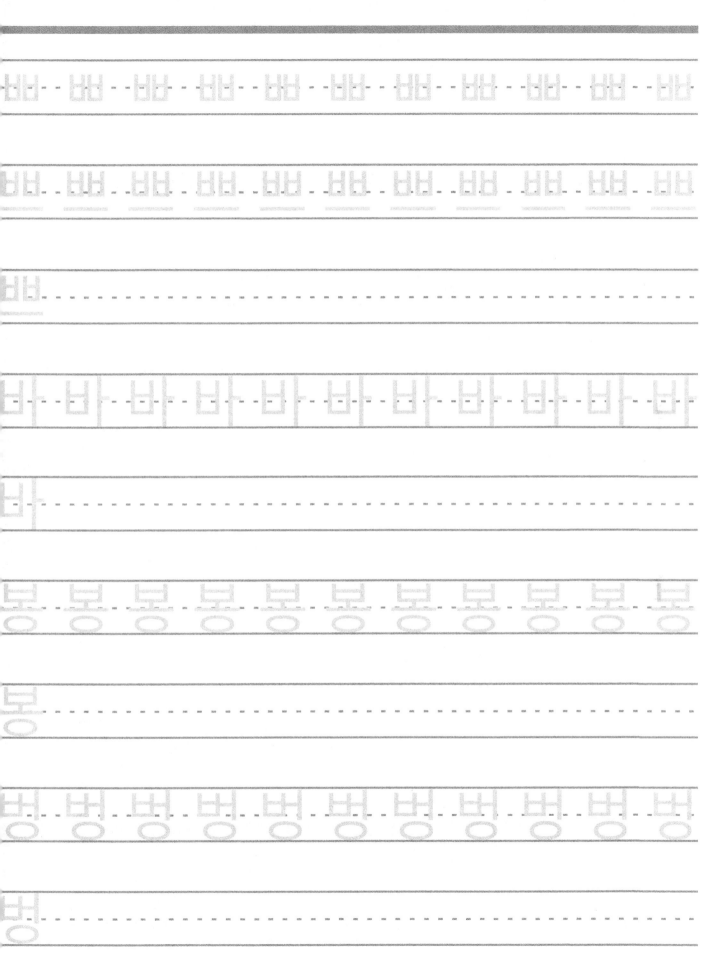

人

시옷
SIOT

S

삼 솬 새
윷 셥 쇄

Approximate Pronunciation

- **INITIAL:** "S" AS IN "SUN"
- **FINAL:** "T" AS IN "OUT"

- IPA: /s/
- IPA: /t̚/

Trace and Learn

人 人 人 人 人 人 人 人 人 人

亼 亼 亼 亼 亼 亼 亼 亼 亼 亼

사 사 사 사 사 사 사 사

소 소 소 소 소 소 소 소

성 성 성 성 성 성 성 성 성 성

Example Font Variations

人
人
人
人

ㅆ

쌍시옷
SSANGSIOT

Ss

1 2 3 4

쌈 쏸 쌔
쌴 썹 쐐

- **INITIAL:** SIMILAR TO THE "S" IN "SUN" BUT WITH A TENSER THROAT.
- **FINAL:** "T" AS IN "OUT"

- IPA: /s̚/
- IPA: /t̚/

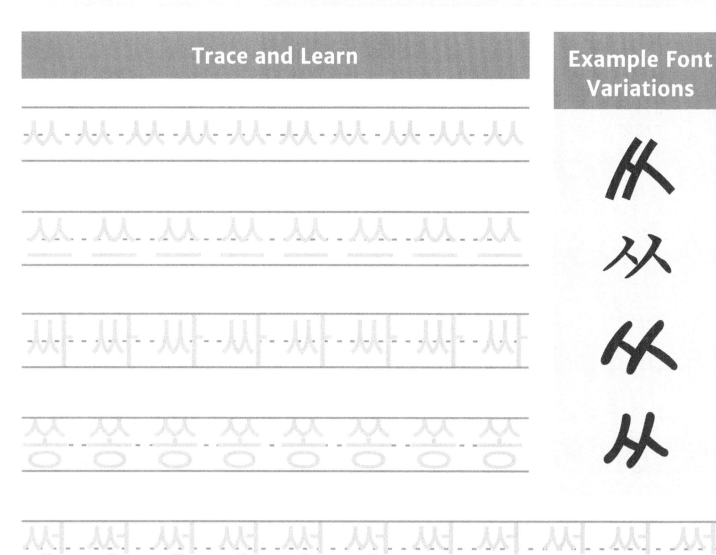

암 완 애
용 엽 왜

이응
IEUNG

Silent

Approximate Pronunciation

- **INITIAL:** SILENT
- **FINAL:** "NG" AS IN "BUILDI**NG**"

- IPA: /- /
- IPA: /ŋ/

Trace and Learn

Example Font Variations

ㅈ

지읒
JIEUT

J

잠 좐 재
쟌 졉 좨

- **INITIAL:** SIMILAR TO THE "CH" IN "**CH**AIR"
- **FINAL:** "T" AS IN "OU**T**"
- IPA: /tɕ/
- IPA: /t̚/

ㅈ ㅈ ㅈ ㅈ ㅈ ㅈ ㅈ ㅈ ㅈ ㅈ

ㅈ ㅈ ㅈ ㅈ ㅈ ㅈ ㅈ ㅈ

자 자 자 자 자 자 자 자

좆 좆 좆 좆 좆 좆 좆 좆

정 정 정 정 정 정 정 정 정 정

ㅈ
ㅈ
ㅈ
ㅈ

ㅉ

쌍지읓

SSANGJIEUT

Jj

짬 짠 째
쨘 쩝 쫴

Approximate Pronunciation

- **INITIAL:** SIMILAR TO THE "CH" IN "CHAIR" BUT WITH A TENSER THROAT.
- **FINAL:** -

- IPA: /t͜ɕ/
- IPA: / - /

Trace and Learn

Example Font Variations

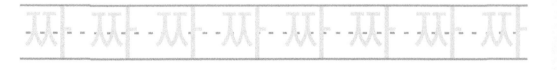

大

치읓
CHIEUT

Ch

참 촨 채
챤 첩 쵀

Approximate Pronunciation

- **INITIAL:** SIMILAR TO THE "CH" IN "**CHAIR**" BUT ASPIRATED (WITH A PUFF OF AIR RELEASED AT THE END)
- **FINAL:** "T" AS IN "OUT"

- IPA: /tɕʰ/
- IPA: /t̚/

Trace and Learn

大 大 大 大 大 大 大 大 大 大

大 大 大 大 大 大 大 大

차 차 차 차 차 차 차 차

초 초 초 초 초 초 초 초

청 청 청 청 청 청 청 청 청 청

Example Font Variations

ㅊ ㅊ ㅊ ㅊ

ㅊ ㅊ ㅊ ㅊ ㅊ ㅊ ㅊ ㅊ ㅊ ㅊ ㅊ

ㅊ ㅊ ㅊ ㅊ ㅊ ㅊ ㅊ ㅊ ㅊ ㅊ ㅊ

ㅊ

차 차 차 차 차 차 차 차 차 차 차

차

초 초 초 초 초 초 초 초 초 초

초

청 청 청 청 청 청 청 청 청 청

청

ㅋ

키읔
KIEUK

K

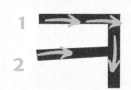

캄 콴 캐
캰 켭 쾌

- **INITIAL:** "K" AS IN "**KEEP**"
- **FINAL:** "C" AS IN "DO**C**TOR"
- IPA: /kʰ/
- IPA: /k̄/

ㅋ ㅋ ㅋ ㅋ ㅋ ㅋ ㅋ ㅋ ㅋ ㅋ

카 카 카 카 카 카 카 카

ㅋ ㅋ ㅋ ㅋ ㅋ ㅋ ㅋ ㅋ ㅋ ㅋ

코 코 코 코 코 코 코 코

컹 컹 컹 컹 컹 컹 컹 컹 컹 컹

ㅋ
ㅋ
ㅋ
ㅋ

E

티읕
TIEUT

T

탐 톾 태
탼 텹 퇘

Approximate Pronunciation

- **INITIAL:** "T" AS IN "TALK"
- **FINAL:** "T" AS IN "OUT"

- IPA: /tʰ/
- IPA: /t̚/

Trace and Learn

Example Font Variations

ᅦ ᅦ ᅦ ᅦ ᅦ ᅦ ᅦ ᅦ ᅦ ᅦ ᅦ ᅦ ᅦ

ᅦ ᅦ ᅦ ᅦ ᅦ ᅦ ᅦ ᅦ ᅦ ᅦ ᅦ ᅦ

ᅥ

ᅣ ᅣ ᅣ ᅣ ᅣ ᅣ ᅣ ᅣ ᅣ ᅣ ᅣ ᅣ ᅣ

ᅣ

에 에 에 에 에 에 에 에 에 에 에

외

태 태 태 태 태 태 태 태 태 태 태

토

37

ㅍ

피읖
PIEUP

P

Stroke Order

Example Syllables

팜 판 패
핖 펾 퍠

Approximate Pronunciation

- **INITIAL:** "P" AS IN "PACK"
- **FINAL:** "P" AS IN "APT"

- IPA: /pʰ/
- IPA: /p̄/

Trace and Learn

Example Font Variations

ㅍ

ㅍ

ㅍ

ㅍ

ㅎ

히읗
HIEUH

H

함 환 해
한 협 홰

Approximate Pronunciation

- **INITIAL:** "H" AS IN "HOW"
- **FINAL:** "T" AS IN "OUT"

- IPA: /h/
- IPA: /t̚/

Trace and Learn

Example Font Variations

훟 훟 훟 훟 훟 훟 훟 훟 훟 훟 훟

흏 흏 흏 흏 흏 흏 흏 흏 흏 흏 흏

흐

향 향 향 향 향 향 향 향 향 향 향

향

얗 얗 얗 얗 얗 얗 얗 얗 얗 얗 얗

얗

헝 헝 헝 헝 헝 헝 헝 헝 헝 헝 헝

엏

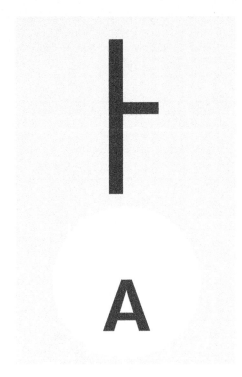

ㅏ

A

1 ↓
2 →

가 깍 낡
닷 딴 랏

- **INITIAL:** "A" AS IN "FATHER"
- IPA: /a/

ㅏ ㅏ ㅏ ㅏ ㅏ ㅏ ㅏ ㅏ ㅏ

아 아 아 아 아 아 아 아

안 안 안 안 안 안 안

악 악 악 악 악 악 악

냐 냐 냐 냐 냐 냐 냐 냐 냐 냐 냐 냐 냐

ㅏ
ㅏ
ㅏ
ㅏ

ㅓ ㅓ ㅓ ㅓ ㅓ ㅓ ㅓ ㅓ ㅓ ㅓ ㅓ ㅓ ㅓ

여 여 여 여 여 여 여 여 여 여 여 여 여

여

오ㅓ 오ㅓ 오ㅓ 오ㅓ 오ㅓ 오ㅓ 오ㅓ 오ㅓ 오ㅓ 오ㅓ 오ㅓ 오ㅓ 오ㅓ

오ㅓ

요ㅓ 요ㅓ 요ㅓ 요ㅓ 요ㅓ 요ㅓ 요ㅓ 요ㅓ 요ㅓ 요ㅓ 요ㅓ 요ㅓ 요ㅓ

요ㅓ

ㅗㅓ ㅗㅓ ㅗㅓ ㅗㅓ ㅗㅓ ㅗㅓ ㅗㅓ ㅗㅓ ㅗㅓ ㅗㅓ ㅗㅓ ㅗㅓ ㅗㅓ

ㅗㅓ

H

Ae

1 2 3

개 깩 넉
댓 땐 랟

Approximate Pronunciation

- **INITIAL:** "E" AS IN "YET"
- IPA: /ɛ/

Trace and Learn

H H H H H H H H H H H

OH OH OH OH OH OH OH OH

앤 앤 앤 앤 앤 앤 앤 앤

역 역 역 역 역 역 역 역

낻 낻 낻 낻 낻 낻 낻 낻 낻 낻 낻

Example Font Variations

H
H
H
H

H - H - H - H - H - H - H - H - H - H - H

애 - 애 - 애 - 애 - 애 - 애 - 애 - 애 - 애 - 애 - 애

애

앤 - 앤 - 앤 - 앤 - 앤 - 앤 - 앤 - 앤 - 앤 - 앤 - 앤

앤

앧 - 앧 - 앧 - 앧 - 앧 - 앧 - 앧 - 앧 - 앧 - 앧 - 앧

앧

H - H - H - H - H - H - H - H - H - H - H

H

ㅑ

Ya

갸 꺅 냒

댯 딴 럊

Approximate Pronunciation

- **INITIAL:** "YA" AS IN "**YA**RD"
- IPA: /ja/

Trace and Learn

Example Font Variations

여
야
여
요

ㅒ

Yae

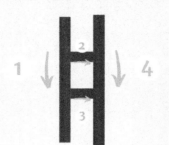

개 꺡 냭
댓 땐 럞

Approximate Pronunciation

- **INITIAL:** "YE" AS IN "YET"
- IPA: /jɛ/

Trace and Learn

Example Font Variations

ㅒ
ㅒ
ㅂ

H H H H H H H H H H

애 애 애 애 애 애 애 애 애 애 애

애

앤 앤 앤 앤 앤 앤 앤 앤 앤 앤

앤

앤 앤 앤 앤 앤 앤 앤 앤 앤

앤

낸 낸 낸 낸 낸 낸 낸 낸 낸 낸

낸

49

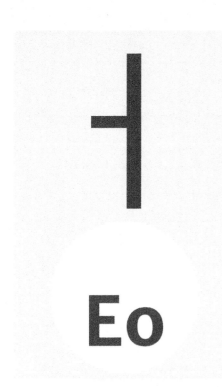

Eo

Stroke Order

Example Positions

거 꺽 넉
덫 떤 렀

Approximate Pronunciation

- **INITIAL:** "U" AS IN "BUT"
- IPA: /ʌ/

Trace and Learn

ㅓ ㅓ ㅓ ㅓ ㅓ ㅓ ㅓ ㅓ

어 어 어 어 어 어 어 어

언 언 언 언 언 언 언 언

억 억 억 억 억 억 억 억

넌 넌 넌 넌 넌 넌 넌 넌 넌 넌 넌

Example Font Variations

ㅏ
ㅏ
ㅏ
ㅏ

ㅔ

E

게 꼑 넦
뎃 뗀 렜

Approximate Pronunciation

- **INITIAL:** "E" AS IN "BREAK"
- IPA: /e/

Trace and Learn

ㅔ ㅔ ㅔ ㅔ ㅔ ㅔ ㅔ ㅔ ㅔ ㅔ

에 에 에 에 에 에 에 에

엔 엔 엔 엔 엔 엔 엔 엔

엑 엑 엑 엑 엑 엑 엑 엑

넫 넫 넫 넫 넫 넫 넫 넫 넫 넫

Example Font Variations

ㅔ
ㅔ
ㅔ
ㅔ

ㅔ ㅔ ㅔ ㅔ ㅔ ㅔ ㅔ ㅔ ㅔ ㅔ

에 에 에 에 에 에 에 에 에 에

에

엔 엔 엔 엔 엔 엔 엔 엔 엔 엔 엔

엔

엑 엑 엑 엑 엑 엑 엑 엑 엑 엑 엑

엑

녜 녜 녜 녜 녜 녜 녜 녜 녜 녜 녜

녜

ㅕ

Yeo

Stroke Order

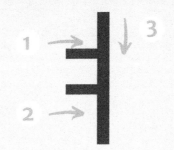

Example Syllables

겨 껵 녂
덚 떤 렷

Approximate Pronunciation

- **INITIAL:** "YOU" AS IN "YOUNG"   • IPA: /jʌ/

Trace and Learn

ㅕ ㅕ ㅕ ㅕ ㅕ ㅕ ㅕ ㅕ ㅕ ㅕ

어 어 어 어 어 어 어 어 어

연 연 연 연 연 연 연 연

역 역 역 역 역 역 역 역

녀 녀 녀 녀 녀 녀 녀 녀 녀 녀 녀

Example Font Variations

ㅕ
ㅕ
겨
ㅕ

ㅕ ---- ㅕ --- ㅕ --- ㅕ --- ㅕ --- ㅕ --- ㅕ --- ㅕ --- ㅕ --- ㅕ

여 --- 여 --- 여 --- 여 --- 여 --- 여 --- 여 --- 여 --- 여 --- 여

여 -

연 --- 연 --- 연 --- 연 --- 연 --- 연 --- 연 --- 연 --- 연 --- 연

연 -

역 --- 역 --- 역 --- 역 --- 역 --- 역 --- 역 --- 역 --- 역 --- 역

역 -

년 --- 년 --- 년 --- 년 --- 년 --- 년 --- 년 --- 년 --- 년 --- 년

년 -

ㅖ

Ye

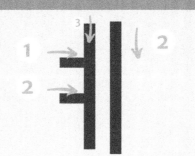

계 꼐 녝
뎻 뗸 롔

- INITIAL: "YE" AS IN "YEA"
- IPA: /je/

ㅖ ㅖ ㅖ ㅖ ㅖ ㅖ ㅖ ㅖ ㅖ ㅖ

예 예 예 예 예 예 예 예

옌 옌 옌 옌 옌 옌 옌 옌

옉 옉 옉 옉 옉 옉 옉 옉

녜 녜 녜 녜 녜 녜 녜 녜 녜 녜

ㅖ
ㅖ
곅
ㅖ

ㅖ ㅖ ㅖ ㅖ ㅖ ㅖ ㅖ ㅖ ㅖ ㅖ ㅖ

ㅚ ㅚ ㅚ ㅚ ㅚ ㅚ ㅚ ㅚ ㅚ ㅚ ㅚ

ㅙ

얜 얜 얜 얜 얜 얜 얜 얜 얜 얜 얜

엤

얙 얙 얙 얙 얙 얙 얙 얙 얙 얙 얙

얘

녜 녜 녜 녜 녜 녜 녜 녜 녜 녜 녜

녜

ㅗ

o

1

2

고 꼭 녹
돗 똔 롯

Approximate Pronunciation

- **INITIAL:** "O" AS IN "BOAT"
- IPA: /o/

Trace and Learn

Example Font Variations

ㅗ
ㅗ
ㄴ
ㅗ

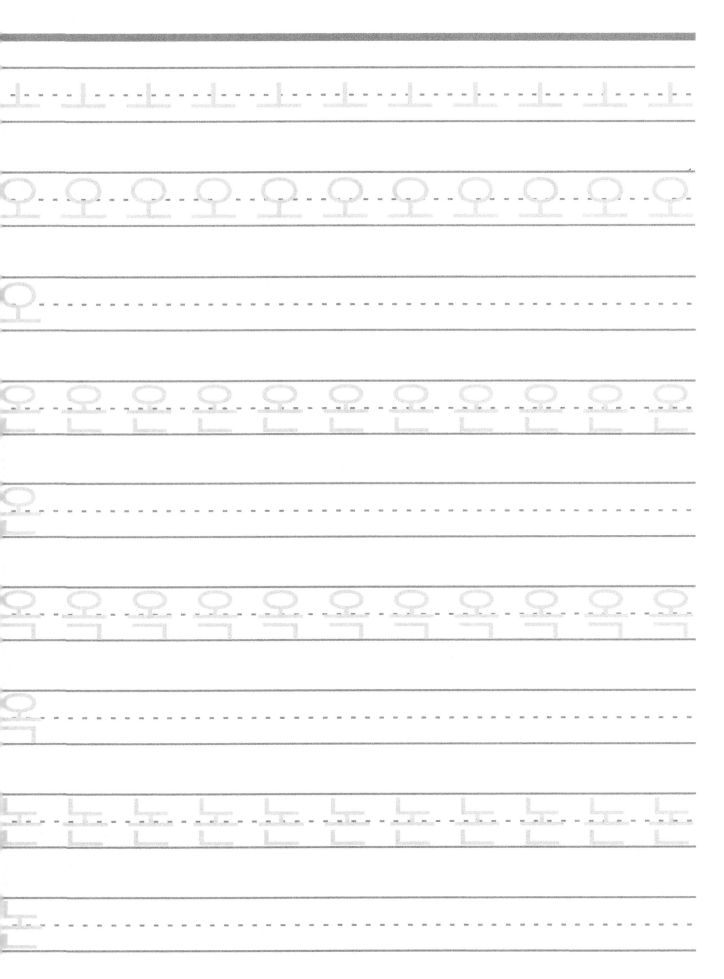

과

Wa

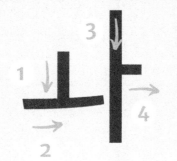

Example Syllables

과 꽉 놁
돴 딴 뢌

Approximate Pronunciation

- **INITIAL:** SIMILAR TO THE "WHA" IN "**WHAT**"
- IPA: /wa/

Trace and Learn

과 과 과 과 과 과 과 과 과

와 와 와 와 와 와 와

완 완 완 완 완 완 완 완

왁 왁 왁 왁 왁 왁 왁 왁

놔 놔 놔 놔 놔 놔 놔 놔 놔 놔 놔

Example Font Variations

과
과
놔
놔

ㅗㅏ ㅗㅏ ㅗㅏ ㅗㅏ ㅗㅏ ㅗㅏ ㅗㅏ ㅗㅏ ㅗㅏ ㅗㅏ ㅗㅏ ㅗㅏ

와 와 와 와 와 와 와 와 와 와 와

와

완 완 완 완 완 완 완 완 완 완 완

완

왁 왁 왁 왁 왁 왁 왁 왁 왁 왁 왁

와

놔 놔 놔 놔 놔 놔 놔 놔 놔 놔 놔

놔

ㅙ

Wae

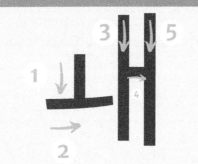

Example Syllables

괴 꽥 눽

됏 뙌 뢪

Approximate Pronunciation

- **INITIAL:** "WE" AS IN "WELL"
- IPA: /wɛ/

Trace and Learn

ㅙ ㅙ ㅙ ㅙ ㅙ ㅙ ㅙ ㅙ ㅙ

왜 왜 왜 왜 왜 왜 왜 왜

왠 왠 왠 왠 왠 왠 왠 왠

왝 왝 왝 왝 왝 왝 왝 왝

놰 놰 놰 놰 놰 놰 놰 놰 놰 놰

Example Font Variations

ㅙ
ㅙ
ㅙ
ㅙ

ㅙ ㅙ ㅙ ㅙ ㅙ ㅙ ㅙ ㅙ ㅙ ㅙ ㅙ

왜 왜 왜 왜 왜 왜 왜 왜 왜 왜 왜

왜

왠 왠 왠 왠 왠 왠 왠 왠 왠 왠 왠

왠

왝 왝 왝 왝 왝 왝 왝 왝 왝 왝 왝

왝

놰 놰 놰 놰 놰 놰 놰 놰 놰 놰 놰

놰

ㅚ

Oe

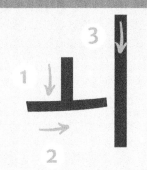

괴 꾁 눼
뒷 뙨 룊

Approximate Pronunciation

- **INITIAL:** SIMILAR TO THE "WE" IN "WELL"
- IPA: /ø ~ we/

Trace and Learn

ㅚ ㅚ ㅚ ㅚ ㅚ ㅚ ㅚ ㅚ ㅚ ㅚ

오 오 오 오 오 오 오 오

왼 왼 왼 왼 왼 왼 왼 왼

욐 욐 욐 욐 욐 욐 욐 욐

놔 놔 놔 놔 놔 놔 놔 놔 놔 놔

Example Font Variations

ㅚ
ㅚ
ㅚ
ㅚ

ㅛ ㅛ ㅛ ㅛ ㅛ ㅛ ㅛ ㅛ ㅛ ㅛ ㅛ

오 오 오 오 오 오 오 오 오 오

요

왼 왼 왼 왼 왼 왼 왼 왼 왼 왼 왼

왼

욕 욕 욕 욕 욕 욕 욕 욕 욕 욕 욕

욕

놘 놘 놘 놘 놘 놘 놘 놘 놘 놘 놘

놘

Yo

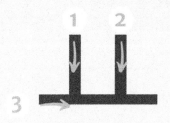

교 꾝 뇨
둏 똔 룧

Approximate Pronunciation

- **INITIAL:** SIMILAR TO THE "YO" IN "**YOUR**"

- IPA: /jo/

Trace and Learn

Example Font Variations

ㅜ

U

Example Syllables

구 꾹 눅

둧 뚠 릉

Approximate Pronunciation

- **INITIAL:** "OO" AS IN "ZOO"
- IPA: /u/

Trace and Learn

Example Font Variations

ㅜ ㅜ ㅜ ㅜ

궈

Wo

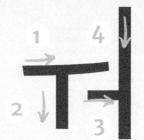

Example Syllables

궈 꿕 눠
뒷 뛴 뤛

Approximate Pronunciation

- **INITIAL:** "O" AS IN "ONE"
- IPA: /wʌ/

Trace and Learn

Example Font Variations

궈
궈
궈

궤

We

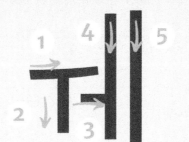

Example Syllables

궤 꿱 눼
뒛 뛘 뤹

Approximate Pronunciation

- **INITIAL:** SIMILAR TO THE "WHE" IN "**WHEN**"
- IPA: /we/

Trace and Learn

궤 궤 궤 궤 궤 궤 궤 궤 궤

웨 웨 웨 웨 웨 웨 웨 웨

웬 웬 웬 웬 웬 웬 웬 웬

웩 웩 웩 웩 웩 웩 웩 웩

눼 눼 눼 눼 눼 눼 눼 눼 눼

Example Font Variations

궤
궤
궤
궤

셰 셰 셰 셰 셰 셰 셰 셰 셰 셰 셰

웨 웨 웨 웨 웨 웨 웨 웨 웨 웨 웨

웨

웬 웬 웬 웬 웬 웬 웬 웬 웬 웬 웬

웬

웩 웩 웩 웩 웩 웩 웩 웩 웩 웩 웩

웩

눼 눼 눼 눼 눼 눼 눼 눼 눼 눼 눼

눼

ㅟ

Wi

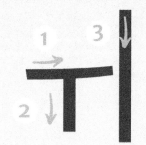

Example Syllables

귀 꾁 눠
뒷 뛴 륅

Approximate Pronunciation

- **INITIAL:** SIMILAR TO THE "WHI" IN "WHISTLE"
- IPA: /y ~ ɥi/

Trace and Learn

ㅟ ㅟ ㅟ ㅟ ㅟ ㅟ ㅟ ㅟ ㅟ ㅟ

위 위 위 위 위 위 위 위

윈 윈 윈 윈 윈 윈 윈 윈

윅 윅 윅 윅 윅 윅 윅

뉜 뉜 뉜 뉜 뉜 뉜 뉜 뉜 뉜 뉜

Example Font Variations

ㅟ
ㅟ
기
ㅟ

ㅠ

Yu

Example Syllables

규 꾹 늌
듳 뜐 릂

Approximate Pronunciation

- **INITIAL:** "YOU" AS IN "**YOU**TH"
- IPA: /ju/

Trace and Learn

Example Font Variations

ㅠ
ㅠ
ㄸ
ㅠ

77

Eu

Stroke Order

Example Syllables

그 끅 늑
득 뜬 릚

Approximate Pronunciation

- **INITIAL:** SIMILAR TO THE "OO" WHEN PRONOUNCING "GOOSE" WITHOUT ROUNDING THE LIPS

- IPA: /ɯ/

Trace and Learn

Example Font Variations

Ui

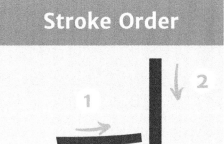

긔 끽 뉙

딌 띤 릮

Approximate Pronunciation

- **INITIAL:** SIMILAR TO THE "G" IN "GO" IF YOU ALSO PRESS THE BACK OF THE TONGUE TO THE BACK OF THE THROAT
- IPA: /ɰi/

Trace and Learn

Example Font Variations

Stroke Order

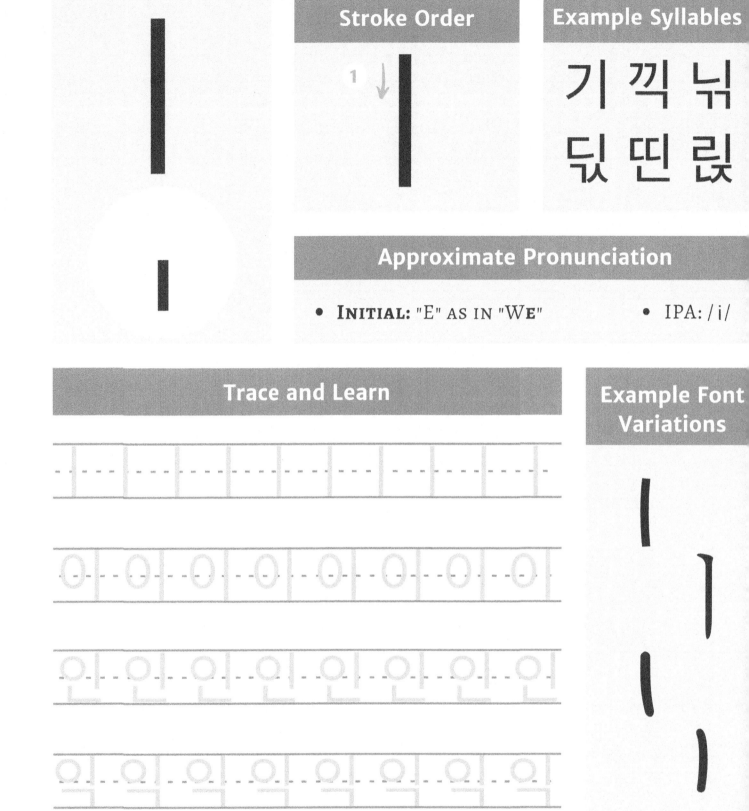

Example Syllables

기 끽 늵

딪 띤 릾

Approximate Pronunciation

- **INITIAL:** "E" AS IN "WE"
- IPA: /i/

Trace and Learn

Example Font Variations

83

에 에 에 에 에 에 에 에 에 에 에

에

에

지 지 지 지 지 지 지 지 지 지 지

지

지

어 어 어 어 어 어 어 어 어 어 어

어

어

것 것 것 것 것 것 것 것 것 것

것

것

ㅎ ㅎ ㅎ ㅎ ㅎ ㅎ ㅎ ㅎ ㅎ ㅎ

ㅎ

ㅎ

있 있 있 있 있 있 있 있 있 있

있

있

도 도 도 도 도 도 도 도 도 도 도

도

도

수 수 수 수 수 수 수 수 수 수

수

수

나 나 나 나 나 나 나 나 나 나 나

나

나

사 사 사 사 사 사 사 사 사 사 사

사

사

람 람 람 람 람 람 람 람 람 람 람

람

람

우 우 우 우 우 우 우 우 우 우 우

우

우

보 보 보 보 보 보 보 보 보 보 보

보

보

ㄷ ㄷ ㄷ ㄷ ㄷ ㄷ ㄷ ㄷ ㄷ ㄷ ㄷ ㄷ
ㅇ ㅇ ㅇ ㅇ ㅇ ㅇ ㅇ ㅇ ㅇ ㅇ ㅇ

도
오

도
오

때 때 때 때 때 때 때 때 때 때 때

때

때

거 거 거 거 거 거 거 거 거 거 거

거

거

갋 갋 갋 갋 갋 갋 갋 갋 갋 갋 갋

갋

갋

주 주 주 주 주 주 주 주 주 주 주

주

주

가 가 가 가 가 가 가 가 가 가 가

가

가

녀 녀 녀 녀 녀 녀 녀 녀 녀 녀 녀

녀

녀

한 한 한 한 한 한 한 한 한 한 한

한

한

알 알 알 알 알 알 알 알 알 알

알

알

쎄 쎄 쎄 쎄 쎄 쎄 쎄 쎄 쎄 쎄

쎄

쎄

령 령 령 령 령 령 령 령 령 령

령

령

99

더 더 더 더 더 더 더 더 더 더 더

더

더

받 받 받 받 받 받 받 받 받 받 받

받

받

집 집 집 집 집 집 집 집 집 집 집

집

집

따 따 따 따 따 따 따 따 따 따 따

따

따

ㄹ ㄹ ㄹ ㄹ ㄹ ㄹ ㄹ ㄹ ㄹ ㄹ ㄹ

ㄹ

ㄹ

제 제 제 제 제 제 제 제 제 제 제

제

제

런 런 런 런 런 런 런 런 런 런 런

런

런

살 살 살 살 살 살 살 살 살 살 살

살

살

저 저 저 저 저 저 저 저 저 저 저

저

저

모 모 모 모 모 모 모 모 모 모

모

모

속 속 속 속 속 속 속 속 속

속

속

만 만 만 만 만 만 만 만 만

만

만

앞 앞 앞 앞 앞 앞 앞 앞 앞 앞 앞

앞

앞

경 경 경 경 경 경 경 경 경 경 경

경

경

중 중 중 중 중 중 중 중 중 중 중

중

중

것 것 것 것 것 것 것 것 것 것 것

것

것

떠 떠 떠 떠 떠 떠 떠 떠 떠 떠 떠

떠

떠

잘 잘 잘 잘 잘 잘 잘 잘 잘 잘

잘

잘

녀 녀 녀 녀 녀 녀 녀 녀 녀 녀

녀

녀

먹 먹 먹 먹 먹 먹 먹 먹 먹 먹

먹

먹

자 자 자 자 자 자 자 자 자 자

자

자

지 신 신 신 신 신 신 신 신 신

지

지

화 화 화 화 화 화 화 화 화 화 화

화

화

원 원 원 원 원 원 원 원 원 원

원

원

Made in the USA
Monee, IL
04 October 2020